REVEREND PAT BARANSKI

The Simplicity of Faith

Part I:

Detroit, Michigan, to
Watertown, Wisconsin

I lovingly dedicate this book to my wife, Ruby—my steadfast partner of over sixty years. Through the long and uncertain days of my submarine duty, she waited, never knowing if I would return, yet always believing that the Lord was guiding our journey. Together, we trusted that God had a greater purpose for our lives. After I gave my life to Christ, we made the difficult decision to leave our families and step out in faith—leaving Michigan with no job, no home, and only the name of a real estate agent in hand. Not long after, I received my call to ministry. Though the news of attending Bible College wasn't easy for Ruby, she faithfully packed up and came with me. We were only there two semesters, but the spiritual growth we experienced was lasting. I returned briefly to submarine service, until the Lord made it clear we were to go to Seminary. Once again, Ruby didn't hesitate—she simply gathered the children and followed where God led. Her unwavering trust in me, and in the Lord, gave me the strength to follow my calling and, ultimately, to write this book. For her deep faith, enduring love, and unshakable support, I dedicate this work to Ruby—with all my heart.

THE SIMPLICITY OF FAITH
Detroit, Michigan, to Watertown, Wisconsin

PROMINENT
BOOKS
EDGE

5830 E 2nd St, Ste 7000 #9983
Casper, WY 82609
USA

This book is dedicated to who that may be reading it out of curiosity, wondering why someone would write a book about himself? Well, it's not. It is about what God did to me and through me because I put Him in first place. The memories I have may be different from other family members and friends, because of the age difference and perspective of growing up, and feeling unwanted or in the way.

This is my story of how God had a plan for me through many years of good and bad religious experiences to personally see myself as lost and in need of a Savior.

There are many people who helped to bring me to the point of knowing my need and lost condition.

The girl with the long blonde hair who sat directly in front of me after our move from intercity Detroit to Dearborn Township, Michigan and her faithfulness in praying for me.

My loving, patient wife, and a pastor in Goose Creek, South Carolina, who counseled my wife and prayed for my salvation.

They were faithful in prayer, eight years after the finger in my face. My wife and children were with me on that Sunday morning.

The conviction started in the church parking lot with the greeter shaking my hand and saying "Good morning. Aren't you glad you're not in jail?" I thought to myself, *oh no, he must have known me when I was in the Heights Men.*

The Rev. Robert Porter: the preacher who gave an altar call. I responded, and as I started down the aisle, I thought the lady across the aisle was that girl who sat in front of me eight years ago. The girl who committed herself to pray for me. I was too ashamed of myself for the way I treated her, I didn't want her to see my face.

I walked down the aisle to receive Jesus Christ as my only Lord and Savior, freeing me from the sins that bound and held me captive to a materialistic world.

I raised the right side of my coat so that the girl from Haston Elementary School would not see how ashamed I was because of the way I treated her eight years before.

The Neumanns, Morgans, Halls, Dows, Angers, Greens, Warrens, and many others who prayed for us and gave us wise counsel. May God bless you, and by God's grace, we'll meet again here, there, or in the air.

THE REASONS FOR WRITING THIS BOOK!

In a world growing more wicked and politically correct by the minute, someone needs to speak up and say the truth and tell what life was like before political correctness replaced common sense.

The Prophet Jeremiah said, "O Lord, I know that the way of man is not in himself: It is not in man, who walks to direct his own steps" (10:23). God has a plan for everyone, it's just that people have other things that dominate their lives. What is first place in your life?

To say that the past two generations lack common sense does not address the failures of their materialistic parents and failing school system. I am thankful to the Lord for His Word. His word was being taught to me by my father. He was careful not to tell me where he was getting it from to avoid conflict with my mother. He would say, "This is what my father taught me. If you want a good life, do what I tell you and you will have a good life."

Because of the prejudice during and after World War II, my father did not tell me that the principles he was teaching me were coming from the Jewish temple my grandfather went to on Saturdays after they moved from Pennsylvania to a city that had a Jewish synagogue. At a family reunion this past July, my cousin told me that his father (my dad's brother) also attended the Jewish synagogue on the east side of Detroit.

My grandfather had passed on before I was born but the stories of his moonshine business lived on for years.

My father was not always the perfect example in everything he did. Drinking moonshine during his teenage years gave him health problems for years. However, the medical problems he had were not understood by me as a kid. My father did not get treated for them until he had to have his digestive system treated because of the alcohol he started consuming at a young age. My mother told me about his prostate cancer and aneurism before he died.

The family, including my father and grandfather, were members of the local Catholic church on the cast side of Detroit. My father never said his dad went to that church.

A book titled *Business Proverbs* contains much of what my grand father and his father were teaching me-sound biblical principles.

Knowing who to believe and who and what to believe in would come in a later date.

There is an old saying, "Actions speak louder than words." The actions of my father toward the priests (at Saint Bridget's) showed that he was not in agreement with them or the way the church did things that I would learn when I was to be confirmed.

This book covers the time period of my life from my birth in Detroit, Michigan, to our departure from Westland, Michigan, to the village of Casco, Wisconsin, and our move to Watertown, Wisconsin.

Someone reading this will say, "What is the point of reading this?"

The point is that God's word stands true.

I was taught biblical principles by my father at a very young age. However, there is a promise by King Solomon in Proverbs 22:6, "Train up a child in the way he should go. And when he is old, he will not depart from it." My father would say "Do right because it is right," which I'll address in more detail. Doing right is what I was being taught.

You are more likely to see people in need-sometimes just holding a door for a lady or someone with their hands full or greeting someone with a warm smile.

A Jewish Grandfather

It was not till years after both my parents had passed on that I found out my grandfather was Jewish. Only once did my father tell me that his father went to the synagogue or sought the rabbis for guidance.

Putting this altogether didn't come until about four years ago when a professor was giving his testimony about seeing what another prisoner had written on the ceiling of the prison above his bunk.

Jeremiah 29:11-14a says, "'For I know the thoughts that I think toward you,' says the Lord, 'thoughts of peace and not of evil, to give you a future and a hope. Then you will call upon Me and go and pray to Me, and I will listen to you. And you will seek Me and find Me when you search for Me with all your heart. I will be found by you,' says the Lord, 'and I will bring you back from your captivity.'"

Through all the near-death situations I had survived and the people who crossed my path and guided me in the right direction and said they would pray for me, I am truly thankful. Putting all of the story together didn't start till eight years after my parents had passed on.

CHAPTER 1

My Beginning

In October of 1946, on a Sunday morning at Mount Carmel Hospital in Detroit, Michigan, I came into the world.

My father's intoxicated celebration was for a weekend or two, according to my mother's complaints, as she told me when I was old enough to know what a drunken celebration was.

Years later, my father explained to me the story behind his celebration.

The Reason for the Move from Their Home near Rouge Park to Inner City Detroit

My father was concerned about a part-time deputy sheriff getting overly friendly with my mother. The man was caught by my dad with his arm around my mother's back. This part-time deputy was also a part-time electrician.

My father had gotten a loan from my mother's father to buy the house in inner city Detroit on Tuller Street. To my understanding, the agreement allowed my father to work off the loan.

Weekends were always fun in the summer as we would go to Orchard Lake. As my father worked off the loan from my mother's father, we would spend the weekends and holidays my dad had off on the farm west of Detroit.

A Close Farming Community

Looking back, I can picture the progress of farming from horses and mules to an army Jeep and to a real farm tractor. The community of farmers did farming together. They started with the spring plowing and tilling, planting, harvesting, and storing. They ate lunch at whichever farm they were working at that day. I know that when they were at my grandfather's. One of my chores was to set the tables for thirty-six farmers at lunchtime in the large dining room or outside.

A Compassionate, Caring Community

The closeness of this community was closer than many families are in the current generation. There was a situation where the parents of a young teenage girl had died in a car accident and of sickness. The grandparents raised her. The grandfather was dying, and the grandmother was sick.

There were a lot of tears. But in front of the community of farm families, she gave her granddaughter to a neighbor. Do you trust your neighbors that much?

I spent a lot of time with the animals. They had quite a variety: mules, horses, rabbits, chickens, ducks, geese, cows, dogs, cats, and pigeons living in the hayloft.

I was given chores to do in the kitchen and the big dining room or outside if it was my grandparents' turn to feed the neighborhood crew.

My grandparents and Uncle Frank taught me how to milk the cows that they couldn't use the milking machine on. Being as young as I was, if Uncle Frank caught me playing with the kittens when I was supposed to be milking the cow next to him, he would aim the cow tit at me and squirted milk in my face. He was teaching me to stay focused on the job at hand rather than the kittens.

One time I was out in the barn in the milking parlor by myself, playing with the kittens and watching them as they ate. I made up a story about a monster in the barn and told it to my grandmother, she said I was quite the storyteller as she related my monster story to my mother.

I really liked feeding the kittens and calves. I liked watching the pigeons until Grandma wanted to eat the pigeons and had Uncle Frank wring their necks.

Several years later, they had to put down much of the herd because of the cows testing positive for TB from the droppings from the pigeons in the hayloft. By then, my dad's loan was worked off.

Years later, shortly before getting out of the Navy, I was given a blood test and found to be a TB carrier. God's protection was there even though I didn't know it. (Psalm 146:9)

CHAPTER 2

The Connection to the Farm

The Story behind the Intoxicated Celebrations

I was about ten or twelve when my father started to explain to me why there was such a gap in age between me and my siblings.

The problem started long before I was in the picture. My father was spending a lot of time at the taverns and pool tables. My mother made some connection with a part-time deputy sheriff/electrician that developed into a long-time affair.

All the things that happened from then till years after their move from the home they lived in by Rouge Park had to do with that when my father confronted my mother after years of drunken arguments. He told me that he told her she had to give him a son before she could be reconciled with him. That was the story behind the twelve-year difference to our youngest sister, the loan, the move, and the working on the farm.

My father explained to me how much my mother's affair had hurt him. The affair continued after they moved. One of the workers who worked with my dad told him he had seen his electrical work truck near our home on Tuller. My dad said he was probably doing some wiring. His buddy said, "He was probably wiring your wife."

The drunken arguments continued until my father caught him with his arm around my mother's back. He said he could arrest my father for threatening a law officer. There were two other stories of them being seen in bed together. After many arguments, my mother agreed to stop taking birth control and have a son by my father. Reluctantly, my mother complied. My mother didn't want any more children after my two sisters and a brother. She agreed to give him a son.

Twelve years after our younger sister was born, I was born.

Other Things That Were Going on in Our Home while Living in Inner City Detroit

Because my father has such a large family, many of which were living in Pennsylvania, I would be left at my first cousins' who lived on the east side of Detroit. When their parents were going to Pennsylvania and we were not, they would leave their kids with my family.

Because of the closeness of age with my cousins, we had more things in common than I had with my sisters and brother.

My Grandfather's Brother

My grandfather's brother who had lived in Pennsylvania and retired from the Pennsylvania Railroad lived with us on Tuller Street.

The story about Uncle Tony that was told to me was that when he was very young he fell out of the high chair and injured his back. His injury made him hunchbacked for the rest of his life. He stood about five feet tall at best. He could outrun me for short distances till I started gang fight training with the Tuller Gang.

Uncle Tony had a few strange things about him. He came and lived with us in the basement on the other side of the piano. The first very stinky memory of Uncle Tony was that he would come up from the basement, sometimes in his long underwear and fix his breakfast in a small pot big enough for a large cup of coffee, a full slice of bread, two raw eggs, and topped off with Limburger cheese. Once the bread was mushy, he would stir it and the smell would empty out the kitchen, except for him. He made funny noises as he ate it.

The second thing was watching kids hit their heads. When he saw younger kids who were old enough to understand money, he would place a coin six inches from a wall and tell one of them they could have it if they could pick it up with their mouth with their hands behind their back. He laughed as they hit their heads on the wall or their noses on the floor.

The Third Crazy Thing

Along this same crazy way of thinking, he would get the attention of a group of youngsters and throw a handful of change, just to laugh at them hitting their heads on one another.

The fourth crazy thing that got him moved to the nursing home was going through everything he could get into when we were not at home and putting peanuts with shells in the pockets of the clothes hanging in the closet. That did it for my parents. They put him in a nursing home.

Little Things That Mattered

Me at our house on 12739 Tuller St.

About the age of eight years old, three little things happened that impacted my life. The first was the teaching of what is now called business proverbs. What my father taught were mainly from the Old

Testament-Psalms and Proverbs-which is different, as the book by that name includes both New Testament and Old Testament business proverbs. He never said where they were coming from other than "This is what my father taught me" "If you want a good life follow my instructions" "Do whatever you do so well, people will pay you to do it again" (Ecclesiastes 9:10a).

Applying the first little thing that my father taught me was how to catch night crawlers and dig for worms. The community was in need of a bait shop. The neighbor next door that owned the triplex, loved her lawn and hated those nasty night crawlers. She wanted us to catch as my father and I could. A few others let me catch night crawlers on their property, and two sportsmen with boats who wanted night crawlers and worms paid me well. At one point, he asked me how many night crawlers and worms I had underneath the back porch. I went under the porch and counted them (It took me a while because I couldn't count very fast). I told him 500. That worked out well, along with cutting lawns, raking leaves, and shoving snow.

To go along with the jobs and bait business, he taught me to be honest: "Use what you have wisely" "Be a good steward of what you have" "If you don't have the money to pay cash, keep saving till you do." At fourteen, I opened a savings account. By sixteen, I started paying cash for whatever I needed. I didn't know how to write a check till after I was married for a year.

The second little thing happened when I was about eight years old. A kid about twelve years old came to the backyard dressed as a Cherokee Indian. He was pan Cherokee and said he would teach how to be an Indian. He taught me where to get the wood to make a bow and arrows, how to harden the tips, and shoot. This fit together well for one of the next major change in my life. Because of his presentation and knowledge of Native Americans, he also taught me how to be an Indian. Making and shooting a bow and arrows was a really good start on what was going to happen.

I did not have a prejudice against Indians. I later married one.

He, however, went from playing with toy cowboys and Indians to a fascination with organized crime such as Al Capone and the Purple Gang. In his late teens to early twenties, he organized his own drug and prostitution business. I can't verify that but that's what I was told by those who stayed in the area.

My mother was not overjoyed in having a little boy to take care of. I was often pawned off on my older sister who is twelve years older than me. This worked out until my sisters started dating. My brother was in school sports, at work, or in college.

My father and me.

The Ice Cream Shop Abduction #3

The ice cream shop, which had an impact on my life, was styled like what we would now call a Dairy Queen and was also located in the Jewish part of town on the next block. I was abducted by a Jewish woman. She was not mean to me. She just grabbed me by my shirt on the shoulder and said, "Little boy, you're coming with me." She took me across Fullerton Avenue and North for two or three houses. She told me she would pay me a dollar to help her clean her house because her family was coming for the weekend. I didn't resent her for what she had done as I had always gotten along with the Jewish people on the next block.

She taught me how to clean her house and behind the furniture, to dust, vacuum, and pick up clothes, and help her with whatever she needed. I did the best I could. Whenever I went to the ice cream store, I would see her looking for me again. That worked out well, for everything you could buy for a dollar back then.

Ecclesiastes 9: 10 says, "Whatever your hand finds to do, do it with your might; for there is no work or device or knowledge or wisdom in the grave where you are going."

An Injury That Changed My Social life

My mother would reluctantly get me up for school, get me dressed, and out of the house, so she could go back to sleep.

I was dressed and out the door running down the alley sliding on the long sheets of ice from the wagons and trucks. I knew I was running late, but I couldn't pass this long wide one. I stopped, went back, got a good running start and about two thirds the way I fell. I used my hands to keep my face off the ice, there was something sharp sticking up that gashed my left hand. I went home bleeding, woke my mother up, and she took me to the doctor to get stitched up.

My First Changing Injury

With every major injury I had in my childhood, it made a major change in my social life.

My injury and healing time changed my activities, and in doing that, I made a new friend. George got me interested in Indian guides and helped me get a job at the same time I was supposed to be at confirmation classes on Saturday mornings which I didn't like going to, anyway. His father sponsored me after many warnings by my strongly Catholic relatives that they might present something that was not acceptable by my mother.

Learning how to be an Indian Guide came easy with what I had learned from the older Indian down the block. It was a really good start. Hiking and going swimming at the Boys Club, YMCA, and doing things with the Boy Scouts was a very good social change for me.

However, this job and dropping out of confirmation classes put me behind on being confirmed when my mother's, relatives, and Saint Bridget's had planned for it.

I went back to classes. I didn't like having my ears and hair pulled or being punched in the arm. I was confirmed. It didn't make me a better Catholic, just a confirmed one.

That was the last major hurt while living in inner city Detroit, Michigan.

After, my mother could no longer have someone else take care of me as my sisters were dating. I didn't understand it at the time, but it was resentment that I was interfering with her social life. As time went by, she would take me with her. She would tell me to play with the neighbors' kids, or sleep in the back of the car if it wasn't too cold or in my aunt's bedroom if it was.

CHAPTER 3

The Neighborhood

According to my brother, the neighborhood we moved into from living on Warwick Street by Rouge Park was a nice neighbor hood. My mother dressed me like a mobster's kid in a three piece suit till in third grade. By the time I was old enough to play with other kids in the community, the neighborhood was no longer how my brother remembered it (that was sixteen years earlier.) Then my brother remembered Detroit.

Detroit, at the time I was living there, there were still cultural neighborhoods. Ours was strongly German. We were Polish but Catholic, so we got a pass from most Germans. Helen, the nice Jewish girl who lived up the block on the other side of Buenavista, was not treated as an equal by a number of the German families. One block over was a Jewish neighborhood, Helen would have been treated as an equal there. I was always treated well by the Jewish people and the British folks on that block.

One block over was a Jewish neighborhood. I was sent to Highland's, a Jewish store, to buy Jewish bread that my mother would call Polish egg twist.

I started kindergarten at Noble Elementary School which was one of the first schools in Michigan to have racial problems that made the news. The truth is, many different races had been coming to Noble Elementary School from Fort Wayne for many years. It was when the neighborhoods started changing that people started to protest at the school for the racial changes in the neighborhoods around Noble Elementary School. I had friends of other colors and races who moved into the neighborhoods or came from Fort Wayne.

Noble Elementary School

I Got in Trouble!

Something happened to me that has gotten me in trouble many times-*blatant honesty*. Around third grade, a new kid came into my class. He was from the Dominican public. He liked to bully me, punch me, and make fun of me me because I was short.

I drew his name for a Christmas present. I did not want to give him anything or have my mother give him anything. I found some old fountain pens, wrapped them in some old purple tin foil, put his name on it, and took it to school. Of course, the teacher wanted to know what me new kid got, he showed the teacher. The teacher wanted to know who drew his name and she said, "Who had his name?" Me, being honest, answered her, "Me." The teacher asked me why. I told her, "Why should I give him anything since he likes to beat me up?" She called my mother and sent me to the office.

There were a number of older kids who had fathers or a grandparent that had been a POW during WWI or WWII and had shared their memories of the war. So, the older Tuller gang members tortured and sexually abused the younger kids of the neighborhood. One time, I saw one of these members coming after me on a bike. I started to run across the street and was hit by a car. The driver stopped but not in time. I was hit in the knee; the older kid rode away.

Gang Training

As I got older, they (the older gang members) started me on gang fight training: throwing rocks and/or green apples, making wammows, and learning how to shoot them. We also learned how to jump from garage to garage. We were having gang fights with the Tuner Gang quite often. I was hit with rocks and green and shot with wammow bands and a pellet gun. Luckily, it wasn't a straight on shot, as it bounced off a garbage can and got me in the side of the head.

A wammow looks like a very large rubber band shooter. The bands are cut to fit the size of the gun you made. The bands were made from tractors, trucks, cars, motorcycles, and bikes with rubber enter-cubes. The length of the center board is how far you want to stretch the band. The second band holds the pressure on the trigger.

Me holding a wammow.

Shortly before our move to Dearborn Township my youngest sister got more serious about her dating. My father informed me that when I turned eighteen; "me and everything I owned would be on the other side of the doorstep on the front porch." He would teach me how to make it on my own if I followed his instructions.

The instructions were taught on weekends when he wasn't working on the farm. He was teaching me more hands-on how-to-do maintenance work: doors, windows, toilets, roofs, gutters, and using basic hand tool.

He told me to be careful who I loan my stuff to. He told me a story about the kid next door to their house on Plumber Street in his old neighborhood. The kid next door borrowed his wagon, went to the railroad tracks, broke the government seal on the door of the boxcar, and stole a large can of lard. It had just started to snow before he loaded the lard in the wagon. The railroad police followed the wheel track to his house where he unloaded it, then continued to my grandparents' house to take the wagon back. Once there, he crossed the yard, climbed the fence, and went home. The police followed the tracks of the wagon.

My father got sent to reform school. While there, the warden taught him to fix his breakfast and how he wanted it fixed: eggs over easy, and bacon, crisp but not burned. My father taught me how to do this. It was one of the other jobs I did when the cooks found out I could cook in Fort Knox, Kentucky.

Over the next five years, my father taught me maintenance skills which paid off in the following fifty-four years. His instructions helped me to set up three profitable businesses, learn a skill trade, plus serve in the military for over twenty years.

Don't Pass Up Free Money!

When my mother figured I was old enough to be left at home by myself, I would sit by the upstairs window and watch the happenings of the community. I took note of the times of police patrols and the actions of the women living in the Triplex next door. Often, the women would give the cab driver a tip of a coin and he would grumble and throw it. I would silently watch where it landed and go out and pick it up after she went in and he drove away.

During this same time period, we were still driving between Detroit and Tipton, Michigan, so my father could pay off his loan.

I was old enough to start noticing what my mother was doing. I asked her about embroidery. She showed me how to do it. As time went by, she taught me how to iron and use a roller press, replace buttons, zippers, and tailor clothes. I found later in life that I had six uncles who were tailors. The training paid off well while I lived in Fort Knox, Kentucky: the tailoring, pressing, shoe shining, and a couple of other jobs I did while being at basic training for the Michigan National Guard.

While still living in inner city Detroit, my mother thought she had found the ideal girl for me. The girl was from the other side of the tracks and a student at Saint Bridget's Catholic School. She had also stabbed me in the chest with an old fashion fountain pen because I had teased her while she was babysitting. Six years later, she enquired at the bakery where my wife worked at about me.

About the time we moved from Detroit, older members of the Tuller Gang were robbing businesses and breaking into homes. At one point, one of the members whose father was a cop broke into a government warehouse, took a swing at the guard, and was thrown. When he hit the ground, he rolled and ran off before the guard could catch him. That was enough for me. I was watching from a distance and didn't want any part of that.

CHAPTER 4

The Move from Inner City Detroit to Dearborn Township

The move was to a closer location to relatives in a smaller house with a bigger yard, bigger garage, fruit trees, and grapevines. It was closer to my dad's workplace and my mother's sisters. We were almost on the border road next to Dearborn, only five blocks from the local school and four blocks from what would become the city hall. The township became Dearborn Heights shortly after our move.

When I started school, the girl with the long blonde hair I mentioned before sat in front of me and started praying for me. I got into sports: soccer and track.

More Injuries

I got two paper routes. I managed to cut my hand on the bottom of the seat of my bike as I was on my way home, so I stopped at the fire department to ask for a bandage. They rushed me off to ER to get stitches. I got it stitched up, and my mother came and got me.

About the time I was getting good at soccer, I got hurt again. This time, it was a big deal. The bleachers were being taken down had over two hundred and fifty stitches between the two legs. I had trouble walking. Once I could walk, I started sparring to practice my footwork in boxing. I sparred with an older gang member. I started going hunting and acquired a twelve-gauge shotgun.

The gang got me involved in various unlawful things that I wasn't comfortable doing on my own. I got in a fight with a gang member who left me with bruised ribs, a broken nose, and a broken collarbone. Last I heard, he got kicked out of the military and went to prison.

That was pretty much it for injuries for me for about two and a half years until I was in the Navy in Norfolk. I was in a fight with three guys. I was winning until I was thrown down the steel steps. I got knocked out but was okay when I woke up.

Back to Gang Life

I had to steal a car to prove I could do it. I did it, drove around, let them off about nine blocks from where I had taken it, and took it back. (It was my boss's car. He never knew I took it.)

They stopped bugging me about not knowing how to steal a car.

The local gang took the name The Heights Men. I joined the gang but never got my gang colors. At about this time, my father didn't like the late-night card games and the guys I was running with. My mother was very much a part of many of the card games. He told me I would be known by the company I kept.

As time went by, I got more into sports, working, and hunting. Shortly before I turned sixteen, my mother was changing the sheets on my bed and lifted the mattress and found an empty whiskey bottle and a twelve-gauge shotgun.

My mother went to Dad and said, "You deal with him."

My father told me I had to take the gun back. He would get me a gun when he felt I was ready.

The Story Behind the *No Guns Near Your Mother*

He then told me why he didn't allow guns like that anywhere near my mother, as he explained to me how my mother acquired a shotgun.

My mother had gotten a twelve-gauge double barrel shotgun that had been involved in a shooting. A couple had been in an argument. She grabbed the gun my mother now had. She threatened to shoot him. He turned around pointed his butt at her and said "Go ahead." She did. My father had a fairly new car, and Mom and Dad went out by the landfill to shoot pigeons. My mother took the loaded shotgun, stood by the car, pulled both triggers, and put a big dent in the car door. The deputies were close enough to hear the shots and came. They took the gun because they had been looking for it from the shooting.

Gun Safety Required

My father said I had to learn gun safety before I could have a gun. He drove me there the first time to the Ford Gun Club to learn gun safety. The following eight weeks, I rode my bike there and back, sixteen miles roundtrip.

Shortly before my twelfth birthday, my folks had bought a cabin north of Hale, Michigan, a mile south of the dance/pool hall where I would meet my future wife.

Between the ages of twelve and fifteen, my father would do repair jobs for my uncle on his lake homes at North Lake and at my cousin's buildings east of Barton City.

While working with my father, my uncle was under the house trying to level it from sliding down the hill toward the lake. My uncle was way under near the middle of the house. My father and I were on the south side outside the crawl space. I watched him hold the jack in place to stop the house from shifting on my uncle while he was being stung in the face and neck by hornets. My uncle got out, they stabilized the house and came back with bug spray.

For a number of years, my father did repairs on my cousin's property just outside of Barton City which had been a large chicken operation.

I had some good friends in the Barton City area and over by the reservation. After I had my driver's license, my cousin paid me to drive his vehicle and trailer from Dearborn to Barton City, but I had to take his younger brother with me.

How to Pick a Wife

About this time, after we came back in the city, my father gave me the *how to pick a wife* lecture. My mother was in the next room, so she could hear him. He said, "First off, don't get one like your mother." She went off. He said, "Don't pay any attention to her. Listen to me." His instructions included domination of in-laws. His instructions helped me pick my wife of over fifty-three years. God had a plan; I didn't know it.

Change of Diet

The Beginning of a Diet of Pizza and Beer

With my father working afternoons, my mother, having her own social life, did not leave a lot of leftovers out. My mother made it clear to me: "Be home by midnight, and don't come home drunk." When I came home drunk, my mother would hit me over the head with a frying pan. She gave the frying pan to my wife. My wife asked me why it was so rounded in the center. Because that was from my mother beating me in the head with it.

I was working, and pizza was only four lots away and it was easy to buy beer. One large meat pizza and a six-pack was a daily diet for me, unless I was with my folks.

Pressure to Leave

I was in the Heights Men. It was humiliating to have a police car waiting at my house when I was walking home with the neighbor girl. Whenever the gang committed a crime, the police were waiting at my house when I was on my way home from school. I would be questioned and released, proving the school would verify that I was there.

I quit school, got a second job, and made an agreement with my father that if he signed for me to go in the U.S. Navy, I would finish school.

I went to the testing room for the test to join the U.S. Navy. I fell asleep before I finished it. I was bummed.

I spoke with a Michigan National Guard recruiter. He explained to me how I could give the guard a try, and then transfer to the Navy if I wanted to.

I filled out the paperwork, took the test, passed it, and got a better job. The job worked out well, getting a promotion, and I was approached to consider management training for what would become Kmart.

I was sworn into the Michigan National Guard two weeks before President Kennedy was assassinated. I wanted to leave for basic training as soon as possible.

I took on another part-time job I could work before I went to my main job.

Months went by, I was going to the drills and training for field communications. I spent much of a Sunday evening/Monday morning losing my whole check playing cards, my mother being one of the players.

I said to myself, "You're being stupid. Go back to school." It was Monday morning. I was changing clothes (just put a clean shirt on) when the phone rang, telling me I was leaving for Fort Knox, Kentucky, in two days. What a time to be in Fort Knox, Kentucky.

CHAPTER 5

The Departure from Michigan

Departure from Dearborn Heights, Michigan, was after two days of goodbyes and best wishes. The train station had a number of crying families for their sons who had gotten their draft notice. A two-day train ride to Louisville, Kentucky, then a bus ride to Fort Knox for in-processing into the army basic training.

It took me about two weeks to figure out how the military system worked.

When I realized how many draftees did not know how to do the simple things that I had been taught as a teenager, I was able to set up a business shining shoes and boots, pressing clothes, doing clothing repairs and alterations, and cooking. I had mess cooked twice before the cooks found out I knew how to cook. It started with breakfast, then went on to the other meals. I checked the schedule to see what I didn't want to do, check the mess cook duty list, approach whoever was on the list, told them my price for taking their mess cook duties, they paid me, then I cooked. I made a profitable business out of what my mother and father had taught me.

I made it through basic training and into on-the-job-training in field communications as a lineman crew member. I had no problem or fear of heights after jumping from garage to garage or jumping off the second story roof of the DPW in Detroit.

What a Time to Be in Fort Knox!

Picture of me in my Army uniform.

I was in Fort Knox at a very interesting time with the Combined Forces Presentations, the filming of *Goldfinger,* and the Kentucky Derby going on in June and July of 1964. That was first time I was around that many state and federal representatives at the same time.

Two of the Same

Shortly before my training was nearing completion, I realized that there were two of us in the same unit who looked alike. Though different in age by five years, he looked younger and I looked older. We even had the same blood type. I could wear his uniform, I just had to memorize his service number. He was going to Vietnam upon completion of training and he had to see his girlfriend back in Columbus, Ohio. So for a generous some of money, I became him for a fourth of July three-day weekend which included military police duty. He made it back on time. I went back to Michigan the following week.

Picture of me in my Navy uniform.

CHAPTER 6

Return to Michigan

I had enough money saved that I didn't have to work between my release from active duty in Kentucky from the Army National Guard to going on active duty in the U.S. Navy.

During that time, I went to the pool hall/dance hall which is now a storage building (pictured on page 19), and found the girl who would become my wife in January of 1965.

On our second date, I proposed to her. She said she was engaged to a fellow in the Army, serving in Germany.

I found out where she lived and went in to speak with her stepfather about why I was a better choice for a husband. It worked; that was what he told her.

We dated: took long walks and built a campfire and watched the sun set over the valley.

Ausable River, MI

I stayed around Hale, Barton City, and Glennie areas of Michigan. A couple of good friends of mine from Barton City had been killed in a rollover after bartering over who could take the big turn on the way to Tawas, Michigan, the fastest. The one fella called himself the Flying Dutchman. The older man with his kid in the back seat did survive, for those of you who may remember him.

When my parents came up to the cabin North of Hale, I introduced my girlfriend as the woman I was going to marry to my father. He treated her as a daughter the rest of his life. My mother didn't like her.

I made my way back to Dearborn Heights where they had a going-away party for me.

Departure from Michigan

I left the next morning for Great Lakes Illinois Naval Training Center. It was a one-day trip that I recall. I checked in, was issued clothes, had a physical, and assigned a company and bunk. I spent two weeks learning naval terminology, then put in a prior service company and worked in the mail department for the remaining six weeks before receiving my orders to Norfolk, Virginia, Armed Forces Staff College.

Departure from Great Lakes, Illinois, to Hale Michigan

Picture of me in my Navy uniform.

I had transfer leave, so I gave my girlfriend that I had proposed to, an official engagement ring to replace the U.S. Army ring. We started making plans for our community wedding.

Picture of Central Fleet Command

From there, I went south to catch a flight to Norfolk, Virginia. I checked in and was sent to the barracks at Central Fleet Command for barracks duty, some mess cooking, then was assigned to Armed Forces Staff College maintenance crew. We did cleaning and polishing work and had duty at the show and library. I was assigned to work for a contractor on the heating and cooling units at the main college building. When that was completed, we installed air-conditioning units in base housing that worked out so well that I requested auxiliary man school which includes installation and repair of heating and cooling systems.

CHAPTER 7

Marriage in Michigan

I requested leave in January of 1965 to get married. The leave was approved, but when it came time to leave, I had to show the chief petty officer that I had the money for a bus ticket. I borrowed the money from my leading petty officer, showed the chief and the chaplain that I had the money, got the leave papers signed, waited till they left, gave the money back, and started hitchhiking to Hale, Michigan.

The trip was slow. It was about 10:00 p.m. when the guy I was riding with got to 94 and 75, southwest of Toledo, Ohio. I was in my dress blue uniform. I walked into the bar, waited till the band took a break, and asked the manager if I could make an announcement. He said I could, so I went on the stage, grabbed the microphone, and asked if anyone was going north. I got to where I was to be at about 2:00 a.m. Saturday.

Ruby and me on our wedding day.
January 24, 1965

Plainfield Township Hall

We got married in the Plainfield Township Hall at three in the afternoon. It was a community wedding; everyone brought something. We were married by a Justice of the Peace. The Justice of the Peace was also a Presbyterian minister. Two weeks later, I let my parents know we were married. My mother was very upset. When my mother demanded to see our marriage license, she noted that the Justice of the Peace was a minister and signed it *Reverend.* She was angry that it was not a priest. She badgered my wife to become a Catholic and be remarried in the Catholic church in Hale.

At one point, the priest threw my wife's Bible at her and told her not to bring it back. On the day of our second wedding, the priest in the confessional booth told my wife the child she was carrying was a bastard. At that remark, my wife reached through the confessional window and slapped the priest on the face. Later, in the fall of the same year, my wife went into labor.

October 1965

The Catholic hospital monitored my son but did not do anything to save him. My mother and the hospital were more interested in my son being baptized as a Catholic than saving his life. The loss of my son hurt a great deal, as my wife and I really wanted him. My wife had fallen down the steps at her mother's house shortly I came home on leave which caused the baby to turn. I had to leave to go back to the base, so I arranged for my wife to stay with my older sister.

After the funeral, I went back to Norfolk, Virginia.

About the same time the US Navy wanted to show off one of their newest ships to the officers at officer training school, so they were all invited to take a short cruse for about four hours. I overheard the offer and I spoke up on behalf of the enlisted maintenance crew being part of Armed Forces Staff College so we were invited. There were only a few of the maintenance crew that went.

Within a few days we were headed out to sea in four foot waves, which did not go well with the soldiers. It was my first and last time of being sea-sick. I was taught how to get over sea-sickness through a conversation with a few crew members within a week of our four hour cruse, I put in for another school related to the four hour cruse. Because of what we would now call fake news, which claimed the ship had sunk because of the poor welding: caused many of the sailors that had applied for the same school cancel their request for the school, so there was a shortage of men for a very hard school. I passed all the qualifications for the school and waited to see which school I would get first.

CHAPTER 8

More Training

While waiting for my orders, I was sent to firefighters' training and emergency rescue training.

This was part of God's plan to save my wife's right eye. I got my orders to the second school I had requested. I got my orders and transfer leave from Norfolk, Virginia to Groton, Connecticut.

I reported to the school, I was part of a class of about one hundred and sixty students. The classes were hard with fast talking on things much of the class was not familiar with.

Another Trip to Michigan

I went back to Michigan for my wife. We said our goodbyes to family and bought a 1960 Ford Country Sedan station wagon with the help of my parents, as they signed for me because I was not old enough to own a car on my own. We went up north to say goodbye to family and friends. We were driving toward Tawas just before the big turn after Iargo Springs when the tie-rod broke. The car went straight.

Iargo Springs

Site of the accident.

We crashed into a tree at sixty miles an hour. My wife was driving. She hit her head and got a cut above her right eye. I got a cracked left kneecap.

I worked my way to the laundry bag which had clean clothes in it. I grabbed a pair of underwear, put snow in it, and put it on her eye. When the ambulance got there, as they loaded us, I was told I saved my wife's eye. We were taken to Oscoda Air Force Base. I was given extended emergency leave. We were able to get enough from the Ford to buy a 1956 Chevy stick shift. It was hard shifting with a cracked kneecap.

We loaded up and left for Charleston, South Carolina. I could only bend the good knee. I had to slide up on the back of the seat to position my foot to put the clutch in to shift. We made there, check in at the base, and looked for housing. We found a mobile home to rent and moved in. Then I checked aboard the ship. I was assigned to the seamen gang until we got underway, then I ran the trash compactor and worked in the laundry room.

After that, I had mess cook duty till we returned from cruise. When I returned from the first cruise, I knew what I wanted to do so I started studying to be a quartermaster. The ship had a great trainer. I started learning and preparing to work as a quartermaster striker for next cruise.

We moved out of the trailer park to the first block south of the trailer park. We stayed there till we left for Michigan.

After out retreat, we purchased a puppy. The puppy turned out to be a very protective dog against snakes coming near my wife and my daughter.

We saw the sights of Charleston Township as we took long walks and learned what there was in the community.

On the next cruise, I worked in control as a helmsman or with the quartermaster on duty. By the end of cruise, I had my practical factors signed off and was ready to take the test. I took the test, passed, and was assigned to another ship.

CHAPTER 9

The Next Big Move

We said our goodbyes, and I got my orders from the captain along with a package to deliver to a ship in Spain. I was given instructions to keep the package close but not to give it special attention. With that and my duffle bag, I was driven to the airport. The plane left Charleston for Washington, DC. Shortly after we reached flight altitude for DC, we started having engine trouble and three of the four engines failed before we got to DC. We landed on one engine. From there, I flew to New York City. I landed in New York but at the wrong airport for my next flight. I had no idea how to get there on time. I spoke to a cab driver and showed him the ticket. He said, "I'll get you there." We were stuck in a traffic jam at Time Square. The driver drove on to the sidewalk to get around the traffic jam. He got me to the other New York airport. I got my stuff checked in and we departed for Bangor, Maine. Once in the air and leveled off, one of the stewards took five armrests out so I could lay down.

We landed in Ecuador. I ate breakfast and waited for the plane to Madrid, Spain. I had quite a wait for the next scheduled flight which would have gotten me to Rodda, Spain, after dark. A B-52 came in with engine problems that was going to Rodda and they worked on it. I asked if there was room for me. They said there was. They had a problem with taking off, but once in the air, we were okay. We landed at the base, and I checked in at transit. I had changed my rank on all but two uniforms. I was told I was going mess cooking in the morning.

I asked if I could call the watch commander. The reply was that I could not bother him at 8:00 p.m. on Saturday night. I asked if I could call the ship I was to report to? He said I could. I spoke with the captain of the ship. He told me he would send his car for me and wanted to speak to someone in transit for my release. The captain's driver was there in minutes. He took me to the ship. I checked in, gave the package to the skipper, he told me to stow my gear and come down to fire control, and he would show me what I had.

I'll just say this: I am thankful that I made it without all four engines failing.

Meanwhile, back in the main land, because I took the B-52, the Navy lost track of me and started questioning my wife and others that I had used as reference for my clearance. We were at sea for two weeks before they stopped the background check. I completed my qualifications for the ship.

I completed the cruse, took my transfer leave and reported to the USS Huntley, which was also home ported in Charleston, South Carolina. My enlistment was almost completed, so I told the U.S. Navy what it would take me to stay in; which was a ship on the North East Coast of New England. They said they couldn't. So I told them I would get out.

While on the Huntley, I got a job at McDonald's for new tires and travel back to Michigan. Before being discharged from the U.S. Navy, I did get my GED from Hale High School in Hale, Michigan.

We left Charleston Heights for Michigan. We stopped at my folks to see if we could use their cabin while I looked for a job. I went to work for a construction company as a laborer for the bricklayers in Tawas, Michigan completing a promise to my father for signing for me to go into the military.

I worked there till we completed the foundation. When it was completed, I got laid off until they had another foundation to build.

The employment agency in Tawas was taking applications for the Ford Woodhaven Stamping Plant in Woodhaven, Michigan. We went south to see if I could work for the Ford stamping plant. I got the job. We bought our first home in Westland, Michigan.

A few months after working there, a fella that went by Little John started talking to me about chickens. As I got to know him, chickens included fighting game cocks, dog fights, drugs and prostitution. Little John was connected to an organized crime organization south and north east of Detroit, Michigan, and including New York. He had many chicken farmers supplying him with roosters, as he had taught the farmers how to train them in preparation for cock fights. I knew more about that then he knew. I didn't want anything to do with that.

I had an interest in metalwork and working with steel. I started trade school at Wolverine School of Trades. I took acetylene gas and arc welding. My instructor, Mike Yhons, took an interest in me, as he had served in the Navy during WW II and had been a coxswain for General MacArthur. We shared a few sea stories.

Work was going well at the stamping plant. I got hurt once that took a chunk out of my nose. I took a test to become a foreman but didn't pass because I would not agree that the general foreman was always right.

The stamping plant changed my shift and I did not want to drop out of trade school. The day I quit Ford's, when I got home, my wife told me she was pregnant. I looked for another job and told the instructor I was looking for a job. He said he would help me find a job that I could work on my welding certification. I went to work at Standard Fuel Engineering near the trade school and Delray. The journeyman; pipe fitter welder, I was assigned to as his gopher—whatever he needed. I had to go for it.

When it came to welding, I literally had to stand on my own welding. I was welding the brackets on industrial ovens. I knew I had to learn other types of welding. I continued taking courses at the trade school which included a course in heli-arc welding.

We purchased a house on S. Vanlawn in Westland, Michigan, closer to my new job at Trio Tool & Die Welding Company, in Livonia, Michigan.

Our house on S. Vanlawn in Westland, Michigan.

I started welding street light brackets that connects the light to the light pole. I started wire welding, then heli-arc welding. That worked out well.

The day shift foreman quite to start his own company in Flint, Michigan. He wanted me to quit and come and work for him in Flint, Michigan.

I became the new night shift foreman while I continued to look for other welding opportunities. I found a job at Garwood Industries. It was much closer, and the job paid well. I started working out as a production line welder, then went to working on custom ordered trucks. This new job put me in a position to see God's Word every day, twice a day, on both sides of the sign, by the road, so I saw it going and coming from work at Garwood Industries. The church had the sign by the with the main verse on both sides of the sign.

Pastor Bobby Porter's Sunday morning message was on I Timothy 2:5, "For there is one God and one Mediator between God and men, the Man Christ Jesus."

The church that had the sign by the road was Community Free Will Baptist Church in Westland, Michigan.

Community Free Will Baptist Church in Westland, Michigan.

The Battle

The Attack on My Wife and Children

A few weeks after I had accepted Christ as my Savior and only Mediator between God and man, we were at my parents' home. My father and I were down in the basement in his workshop talking when my wife was coming down the steps with my son in her arm and my daughter holding on to hand. When they were half way down the second flight of steps when my mother came down the step with her shoe in her hand raised up to hit my wife and children with the heel of her shoe. I grabbed my mother's arm to stop her from hitting my wife and children.

My father watched it all and said to my mother, "You had that coming."

The Sale of our house

I stayed working at Garwood Industries until our home got sold. Because of what I was taught about owning money, we paid off our bills first as soon as the house sold.

The final pay-off of our house in Westland didn't come until we were living in Casco, Wisconsin.

The Trip to Wisconsin

The realtor had shown us a picture of what looked like a nice home in a small town.

The picture was taken of the only good side of the house. The rats had eaten through the other three sides of the house. I asked the realtor what else he had. He took us to the little village of Casco. What else could a young man want? It had a trout stream at the north edge of the property, a small lake across the street. It was the last house in town, three lots away from the school, and six lots from the center of town.

Our new home in Casco, Wisconsin.

Because we lived on the north side of town we were just far enough to watch the Packers on television. The neighbors south of town could only listen to the games on the radio.

We looked at the very large six bedroom country farm house, garage-barn with hay loft and horse or cattle stall, chicken coop and fruit trees and a very large garden on the north side of the house. It was starting to sprinkle when we went out on the north west side of the garden to pray about the purchase of this farmstead. The owner must have thought we were crazy, but he took our offer of our rent being applied to our down payment and paying him off when our loan went through. He accepted our offer.

We moved into our new home.

Ruby, our two kids, my father and me.

CHAPTER 10

Preparing for Our Move to Casco, Wisconsin

We had purchased chickens and were given rabbits from my older sister, the kids had out grown them, but she didn't want to butcher them, so she gave them to us.

We loaded up our pickup and rented a trailer and took our first load to our new home in Casco. The remaining items and the rabbits would come on the last load.

Going through Chicago at rush hour was hard on the chickens, as they stopped laying. We paid our rent towards our down payment and settled in.

(Note the picture on the cover.) I went looking for a job. After a few days of putting in applications we were running out of funds and food. I wanted to have a full tank of gas while we prayed and waited, so I could get back and forth for a week once I got called. We were down to praying for a single egg, so we could all have pancakes for breakfast. We prayed, God answered. We enjoyed our pancake breakfast.

I went for a walk on the other side of town to see if I could get a job picking apples.

I was told by the owner the apples needed a few more days to ripen.

While I was walking back from the south side of Casco, my wife took a call from the cannery in Green Bay, Wisconsin.

The next day I went to the cannery to start my new job at the cannery.

The next day I found out a side benefits of working at the cannery by the pressure cookers: and that was any vegetables or fruit that missed shoot we could have. So, we had our supply of fruits and vegetables all canning season as long as I worked in the pressure cooker room.

The Good and Bad Sides of Working at the Cannery

The good and bad sides of working at the cannery.

The good side was the food, but the bad side was the prisoners that were released for so many hours a day to work at the cannery.

My life had started to change for the better after I came to Christ. I was no longer the foul mouth sailor I had been two years ago, because of God's leading and the wise counsel from the Neumann's and the Morgan's before leaving Michigan. This made me an easy target for the prisoners to cuss and spit at.

So being a Christian among foul mouth prisoners that would cuss me out and spit at me, did not seem like the ideal job, but we had bills to pay.

About the second week I had about all I could handle. The lead man, a very tall, muscular, Native American that had been a U.S. Navy middle weight boxing champion walked with me to the cleaning room the back of the pressure cooker room. He stood about a foot taller than me. He didn't treat me like the prisoners, but just went along with them.

I got fed up, I walked to the cleaning room. He followed me, I was carrying a twelve inch shim wrench. He walked up to me and looked down. I said, "I was not going to put up with this anymore," as I looked up at him with the shim wrench ready to swing if needed. He looked down at me and said, "I like you. You got spunk. I won't let the prisoners bother you." He was a man of his word. Shortly after that the prisoner started calling me names and spitting at me again. The big native picked him up with one arm and held him over the open pressure cooker. He told him, "you do that again and you'll be in it." That was the end of name calling & spitting. I didn't know the foreman was watching the happenings and how arguments had stopped. He had seen the talk I had with the lead man (the big Indian) earlier in the day. He motioned for me to come over to his desk. I walked over to his desk, he was looking at my application.

My Chance for a Better Job

He said, "I noticed you were a welder." I said, "Yes, but I'm not certified yet." He told me, "They are begging for welders at the shipyard in Manitowoc. Check it out, take the test. If it don't work out, you still have a job here."

When I got off that afternoon I gave more thought on the drive home. I told my wife what had happened at work that day. We ate supper and prayed about it.

The following Monday I left for Manitowoc Shipbuilding. I went in and filled some of the paperwork out. The rest I could fill out after the welding test. I waited over an hour. The fella giving the test shook my hand in congratulating me and told me I passed. He asked me how soon I could start. I told him, "Tomorrow."

I found out later that it was the American ship certification test.

I started working with a steel fitter, tacking the pipes in place on the forty-foot booms, and welding the connectors on the ends. I did cutting and learned to use a carbon arc.

The fitter had me get into a steel basket and had the overhead pick me up about twenty feet to weld a boom, I guess, to see if I could handle working out of raised basket. After being a lineman, that was easy.

Back at the farmstead, we were looking into better ways to produce rabbits and eggs. In the process, I found two grocery stores that tried our fresh, processed rabbit meat that passed the meat inspection. The second month, they wanted all we could bring.

Shortly after this, they closed on our former house back in Westland. We went to the bank but the only local credit we had was at the feed mill. We were able to get a loan for the farmstead and pay off the former owners.

The village was small but friendly, except for the priest at the local Catholic church that looked at our last name and demanded we pay the fall drive. I told him we were not Catholic, and we were not paying it. My evenings of kneeling in the mud in my aunt's garden with my relatives to say the rosary were over.

We got to know some of our neighbors. One of them across the road a half mile north was an apple and pig farmer. He asked me to help him castrate his male pigs. I did, and he gave me one. He told me the pig had a stomach problem and to butcher it at about seventy pounds. We placed him in a pen under two apple trees. We found him running down the street being chased by a group of kids. The kid that caught him said it was his. I said, "I don't think so," and took him. I put the pig back in his pen and made sure he couldn't get out. A few weeks after that, he was getting pretty close to seventy pounds. Because one of my relatives got bitten by a pig when I was much younger on the farm, I was somewhat fearful of pigs. I opened his pen and lassoed him. That worked till he saw the corn we had in our garden on to the way to car. I stopped had my wife hold the rope while I got a feed bag. I got the pig's attention with a cob of sweet corn. I threw it in the feed bag. It worked. I took him to the butcher shop and picked up our processed pig the next day.

While living in Casco, I joined the Naval reserve unit in Green Bay which would be a fallback employment position in the future.

My wife caused some resentment because she started a clothing alteration business. I did some repair welding on a neighbor's farm equipment. He was well-pleased. However, the same people that complained about the rabbits, chickens, and my wife's business wanted me to open a welding shop.

Prayer Can Change Habits

I had quit smoking. I didn't think it made sense to be in smoke all day and have a cigarette on break. I chewed tobacco. I had prayed about quitting. I ran out of tobacco, and we went up to Algoma to go trout fishing and let the kids play in the park. I prayed about quitting chewing tobacco. I told my wife I was going to buy some chew. As I turned to walk back to the truck, a man walked up and said, "Here." And gave me a big bag of potato chips. He said, "For you and your family." I thanked him. And thanked the Lord for His answer. That was the end of chewing tobacco for me.

We went to Green Bay to see what it had for churches. We found one that was like the one we had gone to with the Neumanns and the Morgans. We started attending regularly, and I realized I had known the pastor and his wife years before when I worked as a jumper for the Detroit Free Press. They had worked at Ford Motor Company in Livonia, Michigan, before his call to the ministry. We were baptized and joined the church and attended regularly.

CHAPTER 11

The Call to Service

Shortly after becoming members of the church, I was on my knees, cutting the bands of a bundle of eight-foot-long pipes. I heard my name. I looked up and asked, "Soyer, what do you want?" He replied, "I didn't say anything." I put my helmet down and heard, "Pat."

I lifted my helmet again and said, "What?" He answered, "I didn't say anything." I put my helmet down and remembered that Samuel in the Scriptures had to be called three times. (I Sam. 3:4-10) I said, "Yes, Lord, what do you want me to do? The Lord answered me. He said, "You're to go to the hospital in Algoma." I went back to cutting the steel bands.

I went home and told my wife, "We need to pray about something." I told her what happened at work. She knew my feelings about hospitals and medical centers.

I had such a fear of them that before I was married I would hold my breath until I drove past it. The reason for this fear was a terrible sore my father got on his arm from being near or at a medical clinic on his way to work while waiting for the bus.

We prayed about it. After the Sunday services, after we came home, I went to the hospital in Algoma. I walked down the hallways till God let me know which room to go into. I went in and read Scripture to a woman who was ninety-eight years old. A retired school teacher that people of the community had been praying for. I had prayer with her and left. I still remember her last name but I'm sure she's passed on.

After that, I called more often. I remember a call I made shortly before a bad winter storm was already hitting southern Wisconsin and was about an hour away by the time I left the hospital. I walked the halls as I had done before. The Lord said, "Here." There was a teenage girl about fifteen that the nurses were calling the parents to come in because she wouldn't make it till morning. I went in and spoke to her. She was in a bad way. I called out to God to heal her and restore her. I left to beat the storm home.

My wife and I called on her at their home a month later. Her mother asked, "What did you do? They said she would be dead by morning." We didn't hear that she recovered till after the storm. Her recovery had greater impact on the community than we knew.

We had no idea of how her unexpected recovery, the radio ministry, and the New Brethren Church Pastor would bring a revival to the north eastern part of Wisconsin.

We didn't hear anything about it until about ten years later when my wife was having her knee repaired in Rochester, Minnesota. I was talking to a Brethren Missionary in the sauna that told me about the revival they had had in that part of Wisconsin. We drove up there to see the changes in the communities we had lived and worked in. More churches, less taverns, the home we had lived in Casco was about ready to be torn down since it was now empty and not kept up by the bank. It was older then the state of Wisconsin.

"Who hath saved us, and called us with a holy calling, not according to our works, but according to his own purpose and grace, which was given us in Christ Jesus before the world began." (2 Timothy 1:9).

That was the beginning of my calling ministry which I didn't know what that was till the deacon board at Fourth Baptist appointed me as shut-in calling pastor.

CHAPTER 12

The Impact of a Radio Ministry

Pacific Garden Mission

At the time I started calling at the Algoma Hospital, we began listening to a radio program called Pacific Garden Mission. The director would often talk about the name of the church on this dead-end street. There was a bar at the end of the street, he would say: "you have to pass Calvary to get to the Gates of Hell. We all have a choice."

Two college age young men in the next town were listening and called into the radio station and accepting Christ. They did and were told to find a non-liturgical church to attend. The only non-liturgical church had gotten a new pastor, I had spoken of in chapter eleven.

Our pastor in Green Bay had told us if we couldn't make it in to Green Bay, go there.

They went there, joined the church and impacted that whole corner of the state. According to that Brethren pastor I met in Rochester, Minnesota ten years later.

Back at the shipyard things were going great. They moved me to different sections of the shop to work on different parts of the cranes. It was challenging as one day I'd be working on sheet steel a quart inch thick the next day a four inches thick crane body.

After working in the different departments, I must have gotten their attention, as they offered me a position on the assembly crew for the new cranes. That would mean, when I got the phone call I had thirty hours to pick up my plane ticket at the airport and be going to wherever in the world that crane was going. I told the company I needed to talk it over with my wife. We talked about the position and prayed for guidance as to our decision. After praying about the position, I turned it down.

I continued my calling ministry and had a Bible Study in Algoma.

There was a new church start north of Manitowoc, Maranatha Baptist Church, that was meeting in an America Legion Hall. It was where I preached my first sermon.

First time preaching at the American Legion Hall.

Our pastor in Green Bay told us we should pray about going to a Bible College in Watertown, Wisconsin. We prayed about it, I continued to work at the shipyard until the next semester started.

ABOUT THE AUTHOR

Reverend Pat Baranski was born in inner city Detroit in 1946. He is a retired veteran who served over twenty years in several branches of military service: The National Guard, Navy, and the Army.

Pat graduated from Central Baptist Theological Seminary with a Bachelors of Theological degree in 1981. Pat and his wife live in northwestern Minnesota where he is serving the Lord for more than thirty years. He is pastoring a church and is very active in mission work.